32.00

D1604765

Searchlight BOOKS™

Animal Superpowers

Thousand-Mile Fliers

and Other Amazing Migrators

by Rebecca E. Hirsch

Lerner Publications • Minneapolis

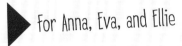
For Anna, Eva, and Ellie

Lerner Publications Company
A division of Lerner Publishing Group, Inc.
241 First Avenue North
Minneapolis, MN 55401 USA

For reading levels and more information, look up this title
at www.lernerbooks.com.

Library of Congress Cataloging-in-Publication Data

The Cataloging-in-Publication Data for *Thousand Mile Fliers and Other Amazing Migrators* is on file at the Library of Congress.
ISBN 9781512425468 (lib. bdg.)
ISBN 9781512431155 (pbk.)
ISBN 9781512428223 (EB pdf)

Manufactured in the United States of America
1-41314-23258-6/22/2016

Contents

Chapter 1

WILDEBEESTS

All kinds of animals migrate. Different animals migrate for different reasons. Some flee extreme conditions. Some travel to mate and have young. On the plains of Africa, more than one million wildebeests roam in search of food. They stampede across grassy plains, swim across rivers, and outrace predators to reach fresh green pastures.

Wildebeests live on the plains of southeastern Africa. Why do they migrate?

Wildebeests, also called gnus, have long faces; shaggy manes; and curved, pointed horns. They look like miniature bison, but they are actually a kind of antelope.

Wildebeests are herbivores, or plant eaters. They fill up on green grass on the Serengeti Plain of southeastern Africa. If grass isn't available, they eat leaves off shrubs and trees. Once they eat their way through the food in one place, they head to new pastures.

These wildebeests feed on grass.

Great Migration

The migration of wildebeests is one of the greatest wildlife events on Earth. Every year, one to two million wildebeests travel across the Serengeti Plain. Under the hot sun, the animals form a thundering herd that stretches to the horizon. Millions of hooves pound the ground. The herds kick up clouds of dust and make the ground tremble. The migration attracts visitors from all around the world.

Wildebeests travel in large groups called herds.

Compare It!

On Christmas Island, near Australia, more than one hundred million red crabs make their own great migration. At the beginning of the wet season in October or November, the crabs scuttle from the forest to the sea. The 2.5-mile (4-kilometer) journey is filled with danger. The crustaceans must cross paved roads, battle ants, and climb down steep cliffs. Once they reach the beach, they mate, drop their eggs into the sea, and return to the forest.

These red crabs are making their way to the sea to lay their eggs.

In eastern Africa, the wet season comes in two waves. Light rains arrive in November and December. Heavier rains come in spring. Wildebeests follow the rains to reach rain-soaked pastures. The wildebeests make their way through the savanna in a big loop. They cover up to 2,000 miles (3,218 km) in a year.

Eastern Africa gets about 51 to 102 centimeters (510 to 1,020 millimeters) of rain each year. Most of the rain falls during the wet seasons.

Zebras eat through the tough grass. Then the wildebeests eat the bits of grass that are left.

Wildebeests travel with about 350,000 gazelles and other antelopes and about two hundred thousand zebras. Zebras often go first. They chomp down the tallest, toughest grasses. Wildebeests follow and eat the tender stubble. Antelopes come last, grazing on the fresh new growth.

The animals have a big role in keeping the grasslands healthy. Heavy grazing stimulates the grasses to grow. Millions of hooves trample seeds into the soil. Animal manure fertilizes the growing plants.

Life on the Move

The migration of the wildebeest is full of dangers. Many wildebeests die along the way. Some get trampled. Others become prey for predators. Lions, cheetahs, wild dogs, and hyenas all prey on wildebeests.

Crossing rivers is an especially dangerous part of the journey. Crocodiles wait to catch wildebeests in the water. The wildebeests crowd along the riverbanks. Then one by one they plunge in. Soon the water is full of animals. The wildebeests that make it across climb up the bank on the other side and continue on.

This wildebeest jumps out of reach from the crocodile's powerful jaws.

WILDEBEEST CALVES STAY CLOSE TO
THEIR MOTHERS FOR SAFETY.

In the southern part of their loop, the wildebeests mate and the females give birth. Predators are on the lookout for young wildebeests. To survive in the savanna, the calves wobble to their feet just minutes after birth. Within a few days, calves can run fast enough to keep up with their mothers. Staying close to their mothers keeps calves safe.

Chapter 2

MONARCH BUTTERFLIES

As summer ends, clouds of monarch butterflies fill the skies over North America. The monarchs are heading for pine and fir forests in California and Mexico.

Monarchs are brightly colored butterflies with orange, black, and white markings. Each butterfly weighs only about 0.02 ounces (0.5 grams), about the weight of a paper clip. Monarchs may be light, but they can travel thousands of miles on their migration.

A monarch's wings reach about 4 inches (10 cm) across. How much does a monarch butterfly weigh?

Migration is a key part of the monarch's life cycle. Monarch butterflies live where milkweed is plentiful. But monarchs cannot survive cold winters. Migrating allows them to escape the cold. Monarchs that live in western North America fly to the California coast. Monarchs from eastern North America fly up to 2,500 miles (4,020 km) to Mexico.

Millions of monarch butterflies migrate every year.

In summer, monarch butterflies live in meadows and fields across the United States and Canada. They sip nectar and mate. It takes about a month for a monarch to go through the four stages of its life cycle: egg, caterpillar, pupa, and adult. Female butterflies lay their eggs on milkweed plants. Caterpillars hatch from the eggs and grow bigger by eating milkweed leaves. The caterpillar becomes a pupa inside a pale green chrysalis. In about two weeks, the chrysalis splits open and the adult butterfly crawls out.

This monarch caterpillar feeds on a leaf.

THE FAT FROM THE NECTAR A MONARCH
DRINKS HELPS KEEP THE BUTTERFLY ALIVE
DURING ITS JOURNEY.

Butterflies that emerge in late summer don't mate. Instead, they fatten up on nectar and head south. As fall arrives, millions of butterflies join the migration. On their journey, monarchs fly high in the sky. They soar on streams of moving air, the way many birds do. Soaring uses less energy than flapping.

On their journey south, the monarchs stop to sip nectar from flowers. After their journey is complete, they won't eat again until spring.

Compare It!

As with monarchs, northern wheatears also migrate a long distance for their small body size. These tiny birds travel between nesting areas in the Arctic and their winter home in Africa. A wheatear is smaller than a robin and weighs less than a slice of bread, making it the lightest of all birds that migrate. Yet it can fly up to 9,300 miles (15,000 km) each way.

Northern wheatears cross oceans, deserts, and ice during their migration.

Monarch butterflies migrate to the same forests year after year. The forests are cool and moist. Thousands and thousands of monarchs fill the forest. They cluster on the trunks and branches of fir trees. The branches bend with the weight of thousands of butterflies. Sometimes the branches even crash to the ground!

Brightly colored wings warn predators that the butterflies are poisonous to eat.

Migration Mystery

Scientists don't know how monarch butterflies know where to go. The butterflies do not learn the location of their winter homes. At most, monarch butterflies live only a few months. The butterflies that arrive in the winter forests have never been there before. Yet this species returns to the same forests each year. Often the butterflies fly to the exact same trees! Instinct tells them where to go. Exactly how this works is a mystery.

Year after year, monarch butterflies follow their instincts to return to their winter home.

Scientists learned that monarchs navigate by the sun.

    Scientists know that monarch butterflies use the sun like a compass. The sun moves from east to west across the sky during the day. The monarchs use the position of the sun to guide them in the right direction.

Journey North

As winter ends, the monarchs in Mexico and California become more active. They begin to fly around and mate. In March, they begin the journey north. Eastern monarchs don't complete the entire journey themselves. Instead, the trip is like a relay race. The wintering butterflies in Mexico begin the journey in spring. They mate, lay eggs along the way, and travel north before they die. The next generation picks up where their parents left off. By summer, millions and millions of butterflies arrive back at their summer homes in the United States and Canada.

Younger monarchs take over from where their parents began the migration journey.

Chapter 3

LEATHERBACK SEA TURTLES

On a warm night, a leatherback sea turtle hauls herself onto a tropical beach. She pulls her massive body over the sand and digs a hole with her back flippers. As she digs, she throws sand behind her. She lays about one hundred white, leathery eggs in the hole. Each egg is about the size of a Ping-Pong ball. Then she kicks sand with her back flippers to cover the eggs.

A female leatherback doesn't guard her eggs. How does she keep the eggs safe?

Each baby turtle is 2 to 3 inches (5 to 8 cm) long, about the size of a cookie.

Next, she hides the nest from predators. She uses her flippers to throw scoops of sand all around the nest site. This makes it difficult for predators to find the nest. Finally, she turns and slowly pulls her body back toward the sea.

In about three months, the baby turtles hatch. They break out of their eggs with a special tooth. By instinct, they climb upward. They wait just under the top layer of sand until nighttime. Then they crawl out and move quickly toward the water. When they reach the water, they swim far out to sea.

Built to Swim

Leatherback sea turtles are the largest turtles in the world. They can be 4 to 8 feet (1.2 to 2.4 meters) long and weigh 500 to 2,000 pounds (227 to 907 kilograms). Leatherback sea turtles are born on land but live at sea. They swim in oceans around the world and search for jellyfish to eat. A leatherback can eat hundreds of pounds of jellyfish in a single day!

Leatherback sea turtles catch jellyfish in their sharp jaws.

A leatherback can dive to 4,200 feet (1,280 m) and stay underwater for more than an hour.

Leatherback sea turtles are excellent swimmers. Their leathery top shell is shaped like a teardrop, a good shape for gliding through the water. Ridges help the water slide off. When leatherback turtles swim, they move their long front flippers up and down. It looks as if they are flying underwater.

A patch of pink skin on top of a leatherback's head may help it know when to migrate. The skin allows light to reach the turtle's brain. The light may help the turtle sense changes in day length.

Leatherback sea turtles don't live in one place. They wander through the wide ocean in search of jellyfish. Every few years, adult leatherback turtles migrate. They swim from their feeding grounds to their nesting beaches in the tropics. They may cross entire oceans. The journey can take years.

Leatherbacks migrate back to the same beaches where they were born. Only females leave the ocean. After mating at sea, the female hauls herself onto a sandy beach, lays her eggs, and returns to the water.

Changes in day length and temperature may signal to the turtle that it is time to migrate.

Turtles in Trouble

The lives of leatherback sea turtles are full of danger. As young turtles race to the sea, raccoons and crabs try to catch them on the beach. Once the turtles reach the water, fish and birds can gobble up the turtles.

Adult turtles face dangers too. They can get tangled in fishing gear and drown. They can swallow plastic trash, mistaking it for food.

VULTURES HUNT AT THE LEATHERBACK SEA TURTLES' NESTING GROUNDS.

Leatherback turtles spend their lives out at sea where people can't easily observe them.

To better understand how to protect leatherback sea turtles, scientists study their migration with satellite tags. By attaching tags to the turtles on their nesting beaches, scientists can follow their movements at sea. One female turtle swam 12,774 miles (20,558 km). That one-way trip took two years. She swam all the way across the Pacific Ocean!

Compare It!

Gray whales are another record-breaking ocean migrator. Gray whales live in the northern Pacific Ocean. They travel to warm tropical waters in winter to mate and give birth. Then they swim back to cold northern waters to feed for the summer. Scientists use satellite tags to follow gray whales. One nine-year-old female swam 14,000 miles (22,511 km). Her trip across the Pacific Ocean took nearly six months. That set a new record as the longest known migration of any mammal.

People can watch for whales in fall and spring as they pass by the coast of California.

Chapter 4

ARCTIC TERNS

Hundreds of small black-and-white birds fill the air. They are arctic terns, and they are preparing to fly south.

Many birds migrate, but arctic terns set the record. They complete the longest migration not just of any bird but of any animal on Earth. These small seabirds fly all the way across the world, from the Arctic to Antarctica and back again every year.

Arctic terns migrate a long distance. Where do they travel?

In summer, arctic terns live in busy, chattering colonies around the Arctic. In the far north, the summer sun doesn't set. In constant sunlight, male and female arctic terns mate. Females lay speckled eggs in nests on the ground. The parents take turns caring for the egg. One stays with the egg while the other hunts for fish.

After the chick hatches, both parents feed and care for it. As the weeks pass, the chick learns to fly and fish on its own.

Parents pluck small fish and plankton from the water to feed the growing chick.

This arctic tern has snagged a fish to eat.

By the end of summer, all the arctic terns must fatten up for the long journey ahead. In September, they must leave the Arctic because food will soon be hard to find.

They begin their journey as the sun sets. For weeks and weeks, they soar over the ocean. If they cross a part of the ocean filled with food, they dive for fish and then continue on. If they cross a part of the ocean with little food, they keep flying.

One way arctic terns figure out where they're going is by following the position of the stars at night.

Scientists have learned that migrating birds use many clues to find their way. When birds fly at night, they may steer by the stars and moon. By day, they may use the edge of continents and the sun to guide them.

Scientists have done experiments to discover how birds find their way. In one experiment, scientists let migrating birds fly in a planetarium, a room with images of stars projected on the ceiling. If the scientists changed the position of the stars, the birds changed direction. This showed that the birds were steering by the stars.

Birds of the Sun

In about two months, the arctic terns arrive at Antarctica. They have traveled to the other end of the world.

When they arrive in Antarctica, it is summer. Seasons in the Arctic and Antarctica are opposite. From June through August, arctic terns experience the Arctic summer. From December through February, they experience the Antarctic summer. Because they live through two summers each year, arctic terns see more daylight than any other animal on Earth.

Adult birds return to the Arctic in the spring. Young terns stay in the Southern Hemisphere for two years while they mature. Then they join the migration north.

Arctic terns shed their feathers while they are in Antarctica.

Practically Pole to Pole

To find out how far arctic terns fly, researchers caught arctic terns in their nesting grounds. They fitted the birds with tiny tags to keep track of their location for one year. The tags revealed that some birds flew as much as 50,000 miles (80,000 km) each year. An arctic tern can live for more than thirty years. Over its lifetime, one bird might travel 1.5 million miles (2.4 million km). That's like flying to the moon and back three times!

An adult arctic tern weighs about 4 ounces (110 g), about as much as a lime.

Compare It!

Like arctic terns, globe skimmer dragonflies are record-setting fliers. They complete the longest migration of any insect. Every year, swarms of globe skimmers cross the ocean from India to Africa and back again. The migration spans four generations of dragonflies. Each generation completes part of the trip. The round-trip is 8,700 to 11,200 miles (14,000 to 18,000 km).

Globe skimmer dragonflies fly in large groups. Sometimes their groups are so big they look like a cloud.

Making the Distance

From birds and butterflies to wildebeests and sea turtles, all kinds of animals migrate to survive. Migrating helps animals find food, stay warm, avoid predators, and give birth. Migrating animals may swim, run, or fly. They may take a short trip or cross vast distances. They complete journeys full of danger. They find their way without getting lost. These amazing migrating animals use superpowers to go the distance.

This baby leatherback sea turtle is ready to start the journey!

Extinct Animal Superpowers

- *Protostega* was one of the largest sea turtles ever, with a body more than 10 feet (3 m) long. *Protostega* lived up to one hundred million years ago, during the time of dinosaurs. Powerful front flippers probably helped it swim long distances to lay eggs on sandy beaches.

- *Camarasaurus* (*below*) could grow longer than a school bus. These dinosaurs walked nearly 200 miles (300 km) across North America. They moved with wet and dry seasons in search of fresh food and water.

- American bison once migrated in huge herds across the North American prairies. Although bison still exist, the giant herds are extinct. A few of their routes can still be seen from the air as deep paths worn into the ground.

Glossary

chrysalis: the hardened outer layer of a pupa

crustacean: an animal that lives in the water and has a hard outer shell. Crabs and lobsters are crustaceans.

fertilize: to make soil more fertile by adding nutrients

hemisphere: the northern or southern half of Earth as divided by the equator

herbivore: a plant-eating animal

nectar: a sweet liquid given off by flowers and used by butterflies for food

predator: an animal that kills and eats other animals

prey: an animal that is hunted and killed for food

pupa: a stage of a butterfly that occurs between the caterpillar and the adult stage. The pupa is enclosed in a chrysalis.

savanna: a grassland in eastern Africa containing scattered trees

species: related plants or animals that share common features and can produce offspring

stimulate: make active or more active

LERNER

SOURCE

Expand learning beyond the printed book. Download free, complementary educational resources for this book from our website, www.lerneresource.com.

Learn More about Animal Migrators

Books

Hirsch, Rebecca E. *Arctic Tern Migration*. Mankato, MN: Child's World, 2012. Learn more about how arctic terns live, grow, and migrate to survive.

Hirsch, Rebecca E. *Leatherback Sea Turtles: Ancient Swimming Reptiles*. Minneapolis: Lerner Publications, 2016. Explore the fascinating lives of leatherback sea turtles!

Swinburne, Stephen R. *Sea Turtle Scientist*. Boston: Houghton Mifflin Harcourt, 2014. Learn more about leatherback sea turtles and how one scientist is trying to help them survive.

Websites

ARKive
http://www.arkive.org
This site from the wildlife group Wildscreen features photos, video, and audio clips of many animals with information about how they survive.

Monarch Butterfly: Journey North
https://www.learner.org/jnorth/search/Monarch.html
Find answers to all your questions about monarch butterflies from scientists who study them.

National Geographic Kids: Animals
http://kids.nationalgeographic.com/animals
Learn more about many amazing animals with facts, photos, and habitat maps.

Index

Photo Acknowledgments

The images in this book are used with the permission of: © iStockphoto.com/1001slide, p. 4;
© iStockphoto.com/Angelika Stern, p. 5; © iStockphoto.com/Humpata, p. 6; © FLPA/Alamy, p. 7;
© iStockphoto.com/AndreAnita, p. 8; © iStockphoto.com/StuPorts, p. 9; © iStockphoto.com/USO,
p. 10; © iStockphoto.com/Jo Ann Crebbin, p. 11; © StevenRussellSmithPhotos/Shutterstock.com,
p. 12; © Ingo Arndt/Minden Pictures, pp. 13, 19; © iStockphoto.com/AttaBoyLuther, p. 14;
© iStockphoto.com/Christian Musat, p. 15; © Giedriius/Shutterstock.com, p. 16; © iStockphoto.com/
JHVEPhoto, p. 17; © iStockphoto.com/David Parsons, p. 18; © Planetpix/Alamy, p. 20; © Konrad
Wothe/Minden Pictures, p. 21; © iStockphoto.com/irin717, p. 22; © Brian J. Skerry/National
Geographic Creative/Alamy, pp. 23, 26; © Doug Perrine/Minden Pictures, p. 24; Al Woodson,
USFWS volunteer/US Fish and Wildlife Service, p. 25; © Mark Conlin/Alamy, p. 27; © WILDLIFE
GmbH/Alamy, p. 28; © Altaoosthuizen/Dreamstime.com, p. 29; © Bruno de Faveri/Minden Pictures,
p. 30; © Arto Hakola/Shutterstock.com, p. 31; © iStockphoto.com/shaunl, p. 32; © iStockphoto.com/
heckepics, p. 33; © Attila JANDI/Shutterstock.com, p. 34; © Aryut Tantisoontornchai/Shutterstock.
com, p. 35; © irin717/iStock/Thinkstock, p. 36; © MasPix/Alamy, p. 37.

Front cover: © Richard Ellis/Alamy.

Main body text set in Adrianna Regular 14/20.
Typeface provided by Chank.